Beauty

In the depths of the human soul, a treasure lies,

A beauty that transcends what meets the eyes,

For within us all, a light does gleam,

A radiance that surpasses any worldly theme.

It's not the perfect face or flawless skin,

But the kindness that dwells deep within.

A heart that beats with empathy and grace,

Shining through the darkest times we face.

True beauty lies in the warmth of a smile,

In the way we go the extra mile.

It's found in acts of selfless love,

In the gentle touch and words thereof.

For inner beauty blooms like a flower,

With every act of kindness, it grows stronger.

It shines brighter than any external charm,

A beacon of hope, a shelter from harm.

Smile

In a world where troubles often prevail,

There exists a magical power, beyond detail,

It's the charm of a smile, pure and bright,

A language of warmth, a source of delight.

A smile, like a sunbeam, spreads its glow,

Across the faces it touches, it continues to grow,

It carries a message of joy and cheer,

Bringing solace, dispelling every fear.

With a simple curve of lips, it has the might,

To light up the darkness, to make things right,

It transcends barriers, it knows no bounds,

Melting hearts, creating bonds.

A smile can heal wounds, both big and small,

It lifts spirits, it embraces all,

It speaks volumes without saying a word,

A universal expression, easily heard.

Diamonds

In diamonds' gleam, a tale unfolds,

Of beauty's secrets, yet untold.

For in their depths, imperfections lie,

A testament to life's nuanced sigh.

Sparkling gems, they're not flawless, true,

But oh, how their flaws reveal a view.

Each crack and blemish, a story untold,

A map of journeys, both new and old.

So fear not, dear heart, your flaws so fair,

They make you unique, beyond compare.

Embrace the scars, the quirks you possess,

For they define you, your essence, no less.

In diamonds' brilliance, a lesson so clear,

Imperfections shine, drawing us near.

Embrace your own, let them guide you through,

For it's in your flaws that your soul rings true.

Dive

In waves of struggle, I dive deep,

Through storms of life, my spirit seep,

With strokes of courage, I push ahead,

A swimmer brave, no fear to tread.

In depths of darkness, I search for light,

Each obstacle faced with all my might,

The water's whispers, they guide me true,

Revealing strength I never knew.

Through currents rough, I keep my gaze,

Towards distant shores, a hopeful blaze,

With every breath, I rise and soar,

Closer to solace, I'm meant to explore.

And as I swim, fatigue may rise,

But hope ignites the fire in my eyes,

For in the distance, I glimpse the land,

Where triumph awaits, with open hand.

With steady strokes, I push and glide,

Embracing grace, with newfound pride,

The shore draws near, my heart aglow,

I've conquered storms, this I know.

Music

In darkest nights when shadows loom,

A melody breaks through the gloom.

Notes like whispers, soft and clear,

A symphony that holds no fear.

When the soul feels lost and torn,

Music gently mends what's worn.

Lyrics, a lifeline, reach the core,

Healing wounds that life once bore.

In harmonies, a refuge lies,

Where broken hearts learn to rise.

Chords of hope and rhythm's grace,

Embrace the broken, mend the space.

Melodies can mend what's shattered,

In a world where dreams are scattered.

With every beat, a chance to heal,

To find solace, to truly feel.

Movement

In the realm where movement's grace unfolds,

Sports become the stories never told.

In each stride and swing, a healing tide,

Where troubled minds find solace inside.

The field, a canvas for the heart to mend,

As troubles fade, new beginnings ascend.

A ball, a racket, or a sprinting dash,

They hold the power to make worries clash.

In motion's rhythm, worries dissipate,

As the mind finds balance, burdens abate.

The body dances, freeing thoughts once confined,

And troubled souls, with joy, become entwined.

Through sweat and effort, fears start to decay,

As sports embrace the troubled minds that sway.

The team's unity, a balm for the soul,

A tapestry of support that makes us whole.

Soul

In shadows deep, where whispers dwell,

I tend the garden of my soul's spell.

With gentle care, I sow the seeds,

Nurturing the essence that my heart needs.

I water it with love and grace,

Embracing solitude's sacred space.

Weeding out doubts and fears that grow,

Sowing seeds of joy, making my spirit glow.

I bathe it in wisdom's golden light,

Embracing truth, both fierce and bright.

Shielding it from the storms that roar,

Building resilience, forevermore.

I tend the garden of my soul's desire,

Feeding it with dreams that inspire.

For in this sanctuary, I find my peace,

Where love and purpose never cease.

REMEMBER TO DRINK

In nature's symphony, a vital chord,

The elixir of life, let it be poured.

With each gentle sip, a world reborn,

For water's embrace, we are forever sworn.

From desert sands to mountains high,

Its crystal essence, never deny.

A river's flow, a soothing stream,

Quenching the thirst of every dream.

Hydration's gift, a shimmering grace,

Reviving our souls with tender embrace.

Cleansing, renewing, it heals our core,

Water's abundance, we should adore.

So raise your cup, a toast to the skies,

Let water nourish, where life relies.

In drops we find our strength and clarity,

A reminder of nature's true prosperity.

Honesty

In a world where truths often hide,

Honesty emerges like a beacon's light.

It stands tall, unwavering and bold,

A virtue more valuable than gold.

With words sincere and actions fair,

Honesty builds trust beyond compare.

No hidden agendas, no deceitful guise,

It uplifts hearts, as love multiplies.

Through stormy trials and uncharted seas,

Honesty steadies, like a gentle breeze.

It fosters connections, deep and true,

A foundation strong, for me and you.

In honesty's embrace, we find our way,

A path of integrity, day by day.

For in its embrace, we're truly free,

To be our authentic selves, endlessly.

Inner strength

In the depths within, a hidden might,
A symphony of courage, burning bright.
Through life's tempests, it takes its flight,
Inner strength, a beacon in the night.

Amidst adversity's daunting gaze,
A steadfast soul, undeterred, displays.
In shadows cast, it finds its rays,
Unyielding, fierce, its steadfast ways.

When doubt and fear attempt to bind,
A warrior spirit begins to unwind.
From deepest depths, resilience defined,
Inner strength, an unwavering mind.

In moments frail, it takes a stand,
A gentle force, yet firm command.
With every breath, it expands,
Empowering the spirit, hand in hand

Mindfulness

In the present moment, gently reside,

Where thoughts and worries softly subside.

Breathe in the essence of tranquility's song,

Let mindfulness guide, where you belong.

Observe the world with a curious eye,

The fluttering leaves, the expansive sky.

Engage with each sensation, profound and clear,

Awakening awareness, dispelling fear.

Let go of the past, let go of the strife,

Embrace the now, the gift of life.

In the stillness within, find solace and grace,

Unravel the beauty, in this sacred space.

With mindful steps, walk the path anew,

With gratitude's whispers, your spirit renew.

In each mindful breath, find your soul's embrace,

Live fully, wholly, in this timeless space.

Appreciation

In moments still, I find my heart's elation,

A grateful song, a humble revelation.

For blessings whispered, woven in each day,

I kneel in gratitude, humbly I pray.

To gentle hands that lend a helping grace,

And tender souls that light my darkest space,

With humble thanks, my heart spills its emotion,

For your presence, love, and unwavering devotion.

Oh, gratitude, a sweet and precious treasure,

Unveiling beauty in life's simplest measure,

In whispers soft, on gratitude's gentle wings,

I soar in awe, a symphony of grateful things.

Opportunities

In life's tapestry, opportunities gleam,

Like stars adorning a midnight dream.

Some arrive with a gentle sway,

While others rush in without delay.

One door opens, another shuts,

Paths diverge, like puzzle cuts.

In each moment, a chance is found,

To rise above or to stay on ground.

Embrace the risk, explore the unknown,

For in choices made, seeds are sown.

Each opportunity, a key to unfold,

The story of life, yet to be told.

So seize the day, with courage and might,

Embrace the challenges, bask in the light.

For in life's kaleidoscope, ever-changing,

Opportunities await, always rearranging.

Humility

In the realm of thoughts, let me dwell,

With open mind and heart to tell,

Humility's grace, a gentle embrace,

Where wisdom's seeds forever dwell.

With ego's mask, I shall not wear,

For open minds can truly dare,

To listen, learn, and comprehend,

The beauty in perspectives shared.

For in humility's tender embrace,

We find the strength to set our pace,

To welcome new horizons wide,

With open hearts, side by side.

Acceptance

In a world diverse, we find our place,

Where acceptance blooms, with gentle grace.

For in embracing differences, we see,

The beauty that lies in you and me.

A tapestry woven, colors unite,

Each thread weaves a story, shining bright.

No judgment or fear can cloud our sight,

Acceptance brings harmony, day and night.

With open hearts, we break down the walls,

Embracing the unique, as each soul calls.

For in acceptance, true freedom's found,

A bond of compassion, strong and profound.

Thank you for reading

Joakim Nurminen

Kustantaja: BoD – Books on Demand, Helsinki, Suomi

Valmistaja: BoD – Books on Demand, Norderstedt, Saksa

ISBN: 978-952-80-0297-0